The Rendition of Souls

By

R. C. Webb

Black Cat Publishing

Dark Home of the New Surrealism

San Miguel de Allende, Mexico

The Rendition of Souls

Plate 1 Haji-Badji Road Trip

A spirit guide named Wah-Too-Se takes Hadji-Badjis on their Haj to the Edge of Tomorrow.

It is a sacred place and only the pure of heart may go there. It is a treacherous journey through, with abandoned mine shafts full of hungry mush hunting glow-in-the-dark Nightwalkers and other evil like Coyote and his army of Perves.

On a high mesa overlooking the scorched Valley of No dwells the oracle No-NA-Me. She is the sky daughter of Hermorpho and Dytee. She can smell a rat even before the rat smells itself, thereby thwarting, with talismans, curses, and hexes, the soul-sucking mischief of the ratty Perves, as well as the assaults of the bone crushing Nightwalkers.

The Nightwalkers are radioactive mutants condemned to the dark who are castaways to the abandoned mineshafts of The Wasteland. Generally, they come out at night for fresh road kill but have no qualms about gnarling a Hadji-Badji or two, or three, who are usually too stoned on "Night Air" to put up any resistance. No arms or heads doesn't help them very much either.

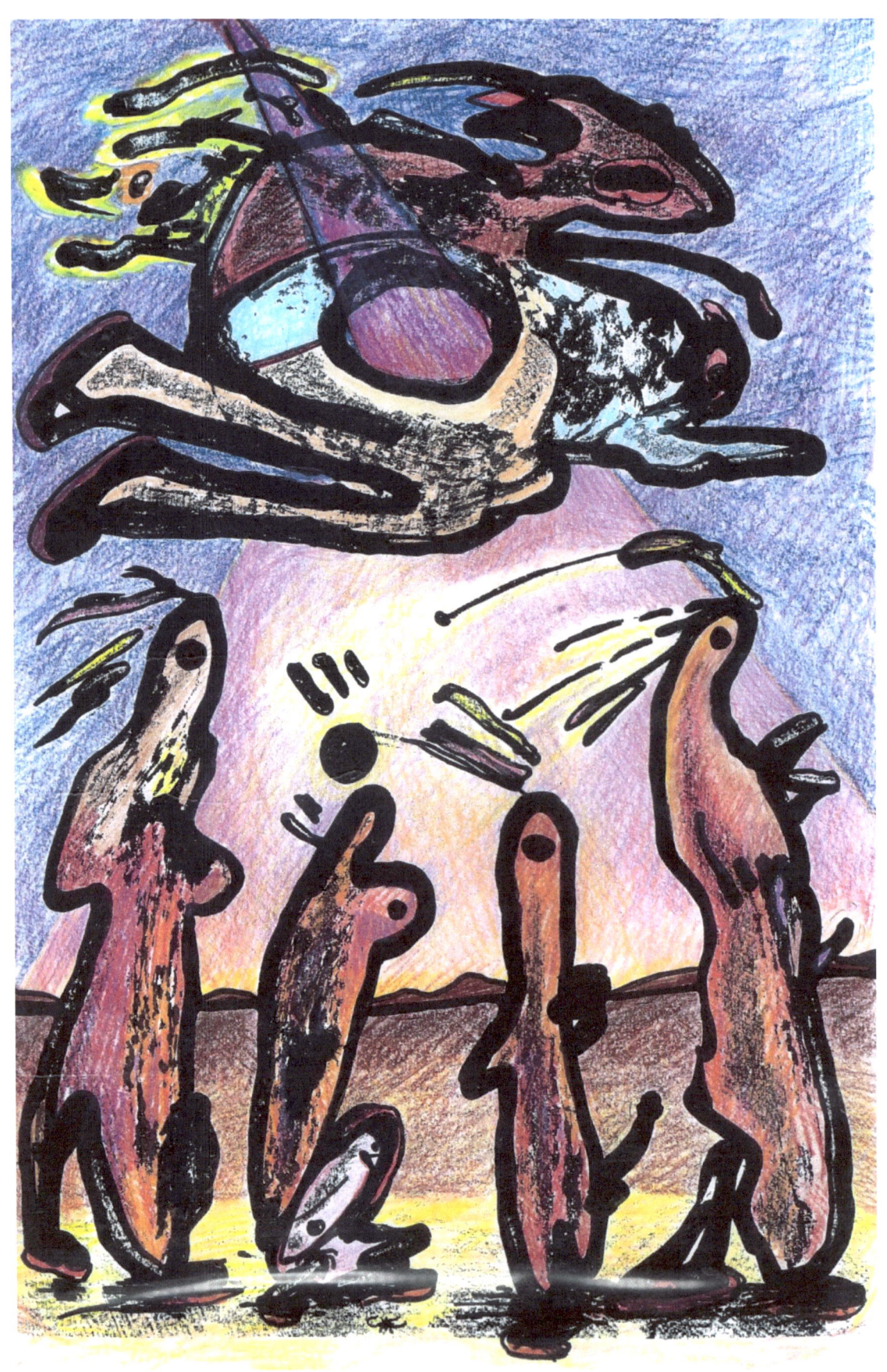

The Perves are a gang of shape-shifting mercenary soul bangers led by Coyote, whose favorite pastime is preying on the Anthropomorphic Hadji-Badjis, as they are called, making their way through the Wasteland to the high mesa hooch of No-Na-Me and her Astral Clinic for Radical Colon Realignment, which was thought to cure just about everything standing in the way of unfettered enlightenment.

No-Na-Me is instrumental in the performance of No Sex, Same Sex, and Bad Sex marriages that are so important to Anthropomorphos and their compromised love life.

Coyote despises No-Na-Me and her tribe and is ruthless in his acquisition of their Souls, which he uses for barter with "three legged preachers in two legged pants" and, of course, the bastard son of Red Riding Hood: Coupe De Vil.

Saca-Jah-Wee-Ah is an herb that Coyote loves. It is a cross between peyote and psilocybin. Coupe De Vil and The Priest called Father Bendover always seem to have the only sanctified stash, which they gladly trade for souls. Coup De Vil likes Girl Scout souls and Father Bendover, of course, likes Boy Scout souls.

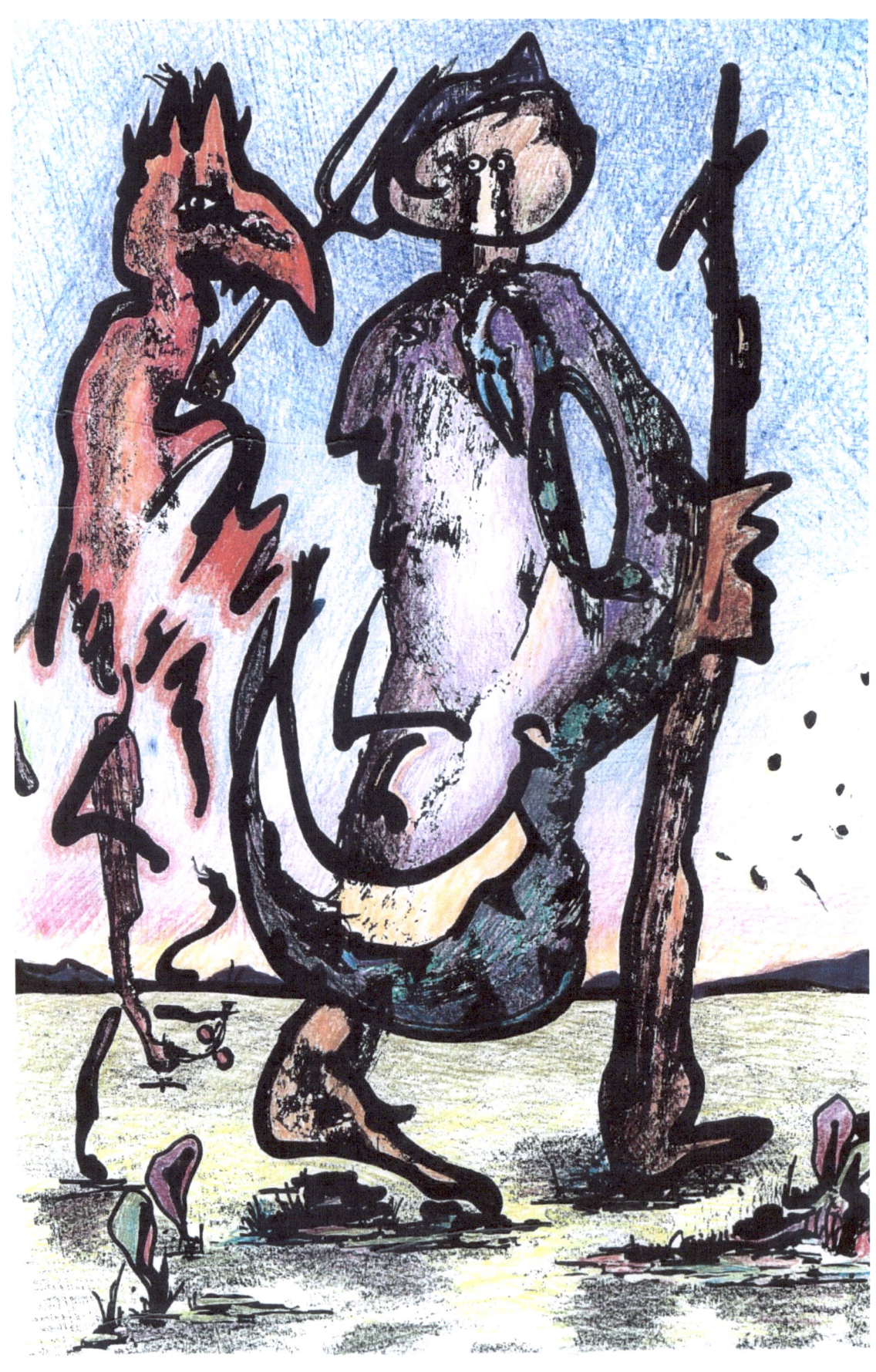

Plate 2: Da Deal

With a fresh expedition of Hadji-Badji Souls headed for the Oracle of No-Na-Me, Coup De Vil makes a deal with the Boy Boffer clergy of the 4th Reich, Father Bendover.

For the Priest, 2 quasi males: Yow-za and Yo-Ma-Ma. And for Coup De Vil, 2 quasi Fems: Sez Schwan and Gol-Di-Gah, all ready for some serious shape-shifting debauchery.

The problem is that neither Coup De Vil nor Father Bendover possesses the power, due to biblical restraints, to entrap these particular pilgrims. Their Saca-Jah-Wee-Ah stash, on the other hand, was quite large.

For their scorched desert Doo-Bad, none other than Coyote and the Perves would do.

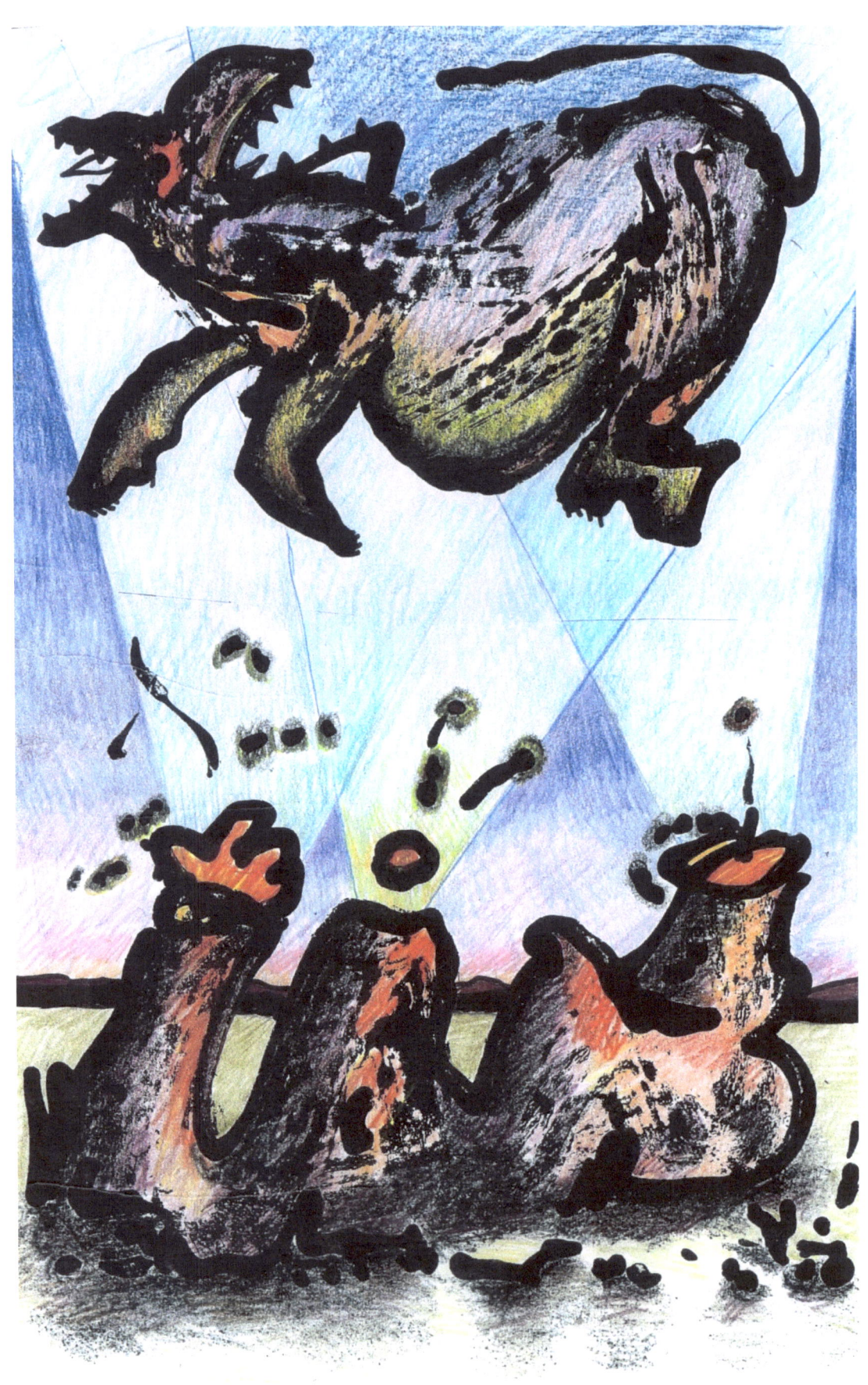

Plate 3: Coyote Conjured

Coup De Vil and Father Bendover, using an old Sodom and Gomorrah "Come Hither" ritual called "Rub Yo Dicks Together" is used to conjure up the army of assholes. The ritual is a passionless exercise in male demagoguery for tricking the Perves from their subterranean lair with the promise of Saca-Jah-Wee-Ah and other earthly delights.

From the bowels (P.U.!) of the blackened earth, Coyote and his minions rise up ready to do some serious damage to Na-Na-Me and her so called Divinity.

Being a Coyote, with many young to feed, he is not about to take charge of the Rendition of Souls without getting his Saca-Jah-Wee-Ah out front. He has not respect, nor does he trust, these two whores of Heaven and Hell.

The Price? Let's see now…. One pound per pecker times 2 and One and a half pounds per puss (more fun) times two equals seven pounds of Sacah-Jah-Wee-Ah. Da Deal is cut!

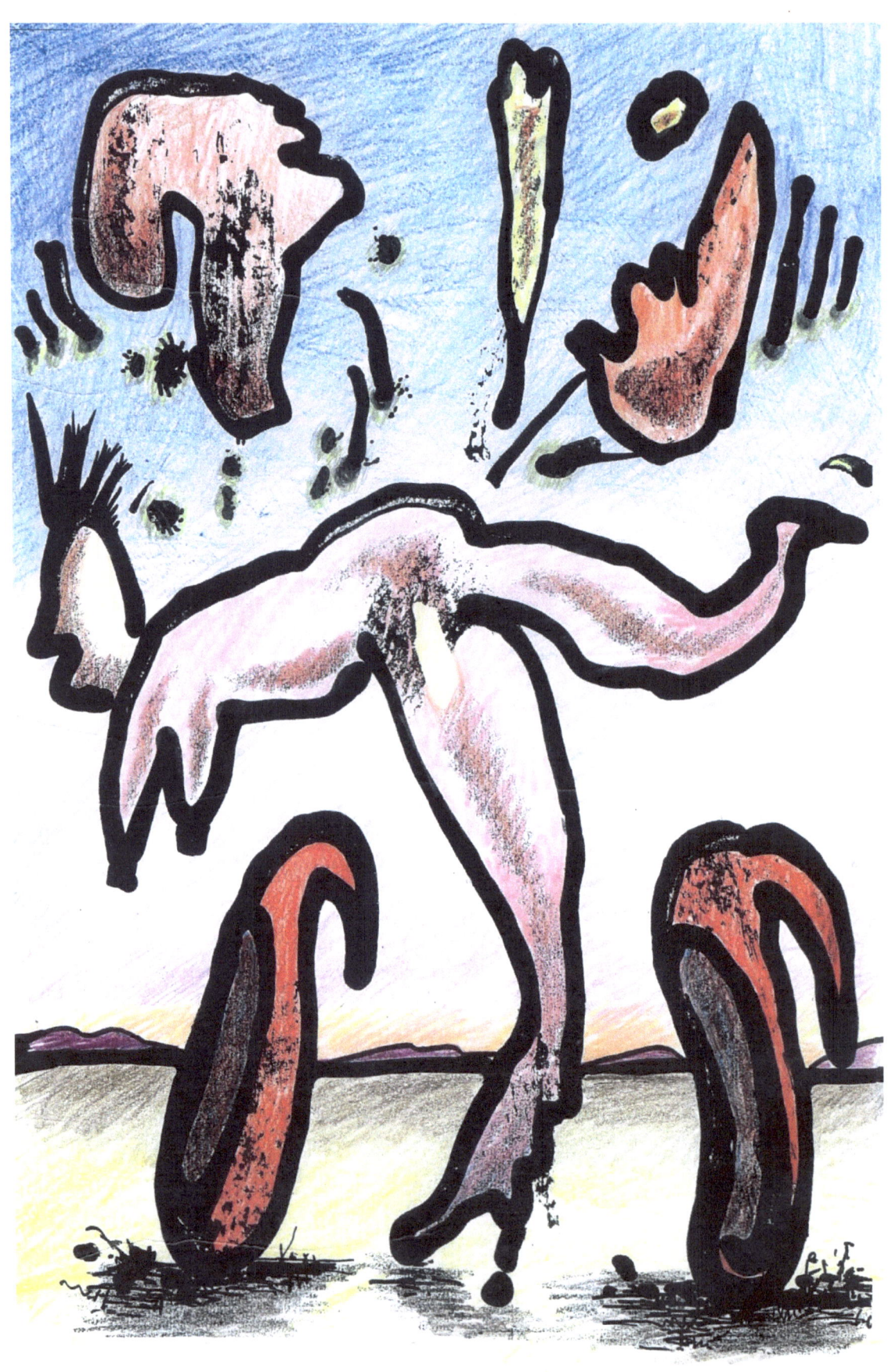

Plate 4: The Trickster

Being more aligned with Coup De Vil than the stuffy Father Bendover, Coyote starts in on the youngest Hadji-Badji named Gol-Di-Gah. Using highly suggestive cloud formations and concealed puffs of Saca-Jah-Wee-Ah directed toward her, she starts to feel Strange.

Temptation for earthly wonders, paraded by that scoundrel Coyote, begins to grow. Since feet are the only real appendage of the Anthros, their inability to resist a pair of Hot Red Shoes is of no wonder. The sound of a couple of wagon loads of Par-Te-Har-Tes just over the dune is too much for Gol-Di-Gah! With the Hot Red Shoes she surrenders her Soul and treks off to Boo-gee stumbling and staggering in the sand toward what turned out to be just a boom-box with a soundtrack tape from Animal House! This was Coyote's version of romance. First trick'em, then Dick 'em.

"Coyote, you Asshole!" weeps the Soulless Hadji-Badji, the red shoes, just an illusion, return to their pre-deception state as a pair of donkey crap covered huaraches.

Coyote stuffs her Soul into his Doo-Bad gunny sack and heads back to the campsite where Sez Schwan is taking a nap up against a soft rock next to the twinkling fire.

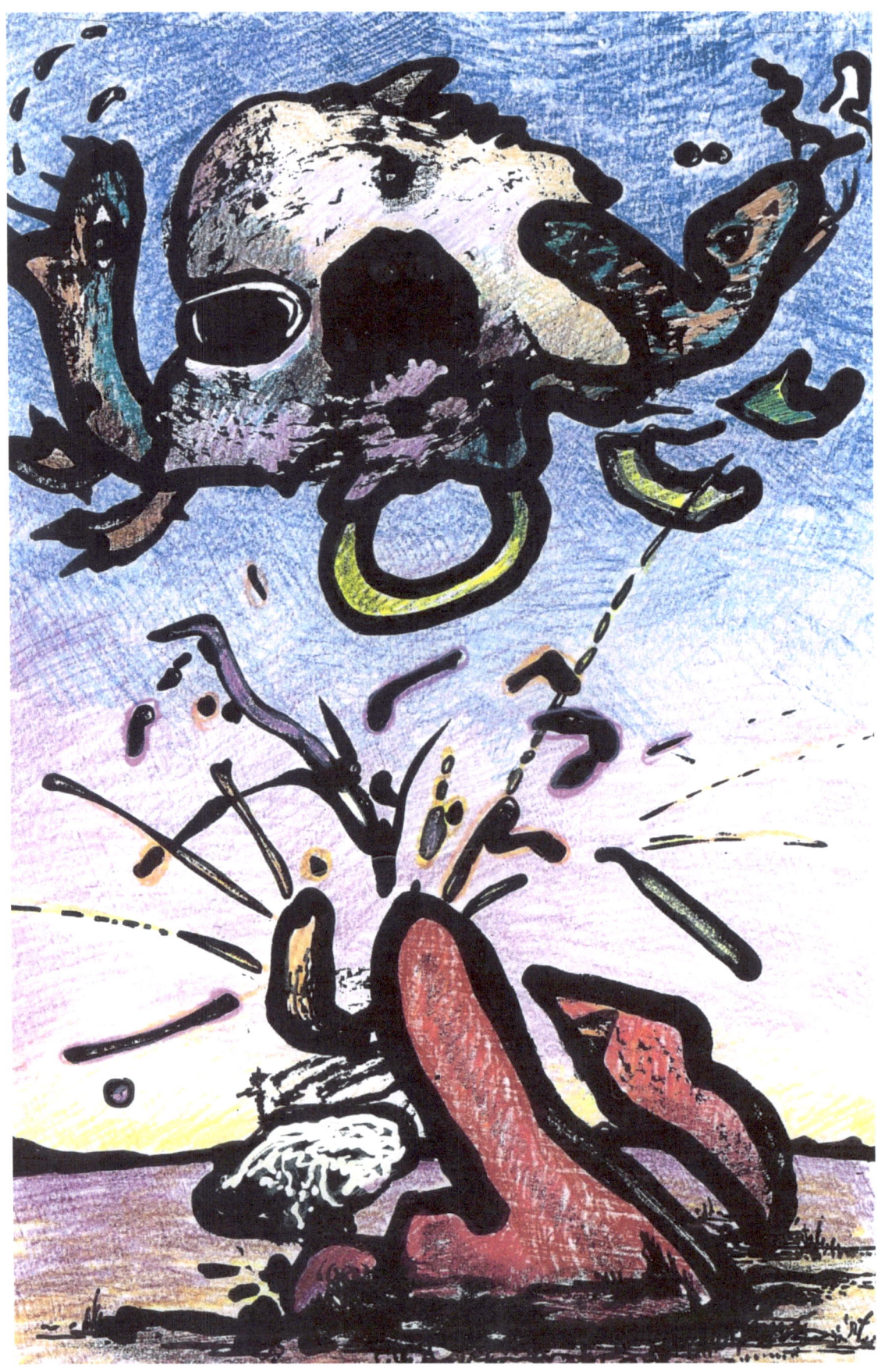

Plate 5: Swan Song

As part of the deal, Coyote gets to keep the mortal version of his catch to do what he will with. While the Perves are known for their nonexistent standards, Coyote decries the headless, armless, and humorless Hadji-Badjis as big "turnoffs." His bad luck BooZoo with Gol-Di-Gah was surely evidence of that!

Sez Schwan was more mature than her girlfriend and would never fall for the Red Shoes routine. To BooZoo her, Coyote must sneak up on her in a dream state and shift her into his favorite Big Bird. A beautiful succulent Swan turning his sandbox into a cool oasis already named for a fiery Chinese cuisine!

Getting down to the "Business of Isness," Coyote knows Sez Schwan, now spelled "Swan," will not go EZ. If she wakes before the Shift is complete, she will walk the earth as a lonely Morh, neither Anthropo nor Poid, with a worthless, tortured Soul.

Coyote calls on the White god of Old Men named Sky Turtle to conjure up an old Hopi snapping turtle/rattle snake pecker pumping conjuration designed for performance anxiety between boring Anthros and over-complicated libidos of the Coyote Clans.

From the cloud above drops the proverbial gold plated cock ring guaranteed, when properly affixed, to produce the ass-breaking version of bad sex with Infidels.

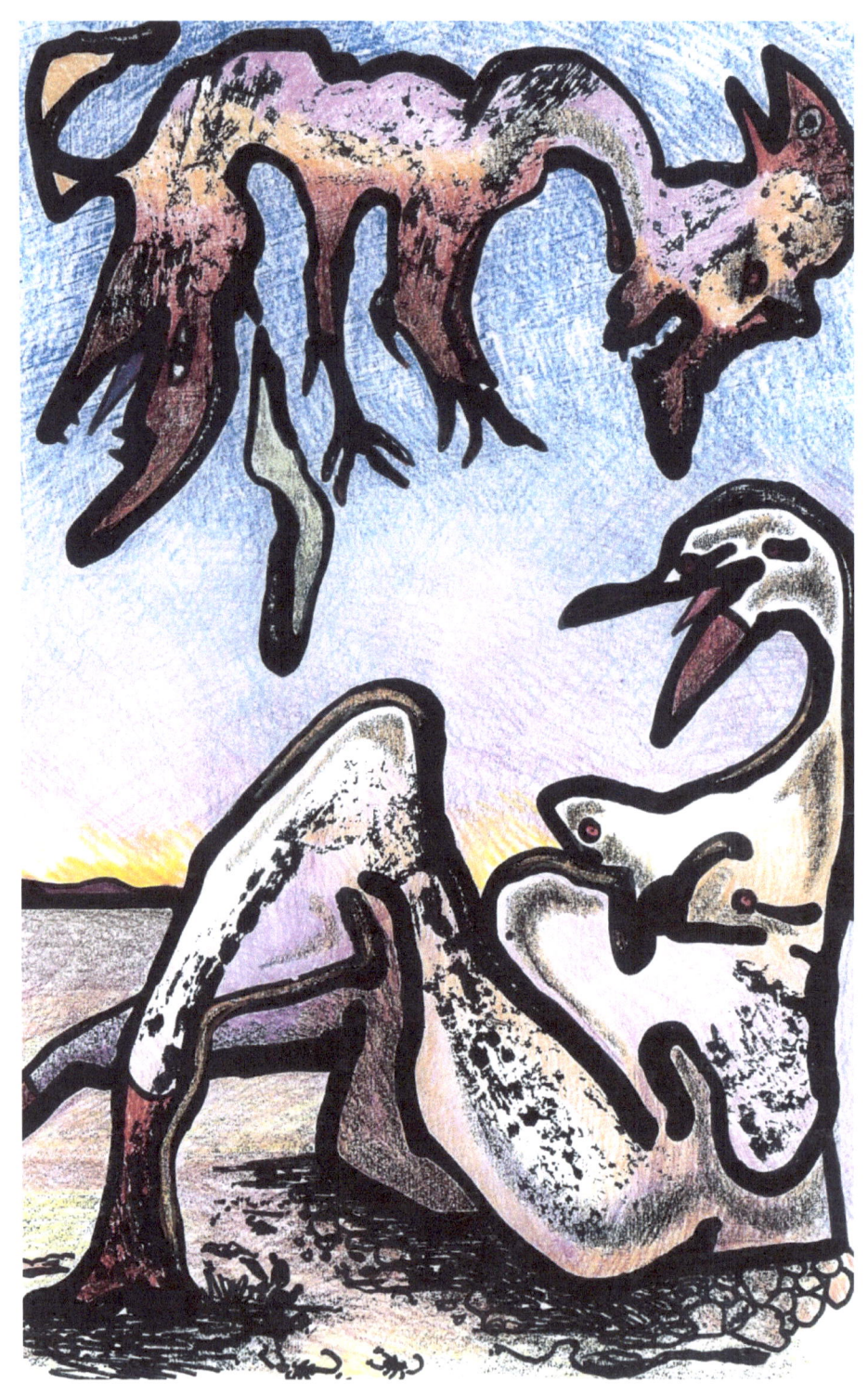

Plate 6: Pig at Heart

Sez Schwan, now Sez Swan, still sleeping, dreams of the beautiful lake on the high mesa and her coming visit with her beloved No-Na-Me.

Being a PIG at Heart, Coyote decides to loosen up the sleeping Sez Swan with a little shower of affection. Sez Swan is awakened by the millions of little Coyote seeds being dumped on her earthly garden.

Caught off-guard and stunned by her new feathery fame, Coyote snatches Sez Swan's Soul as it leaves like yesterday's freight train in an attempt to escape the treachery of this dirty pig-dog!

Sez Swan's Soul is shoved into the waiting gunny sack with Gol-Di-Gah, and like a bag of Cats they romp and chomp in their burlap cage in the dark, howling like Banshees and Demons of the Gale!

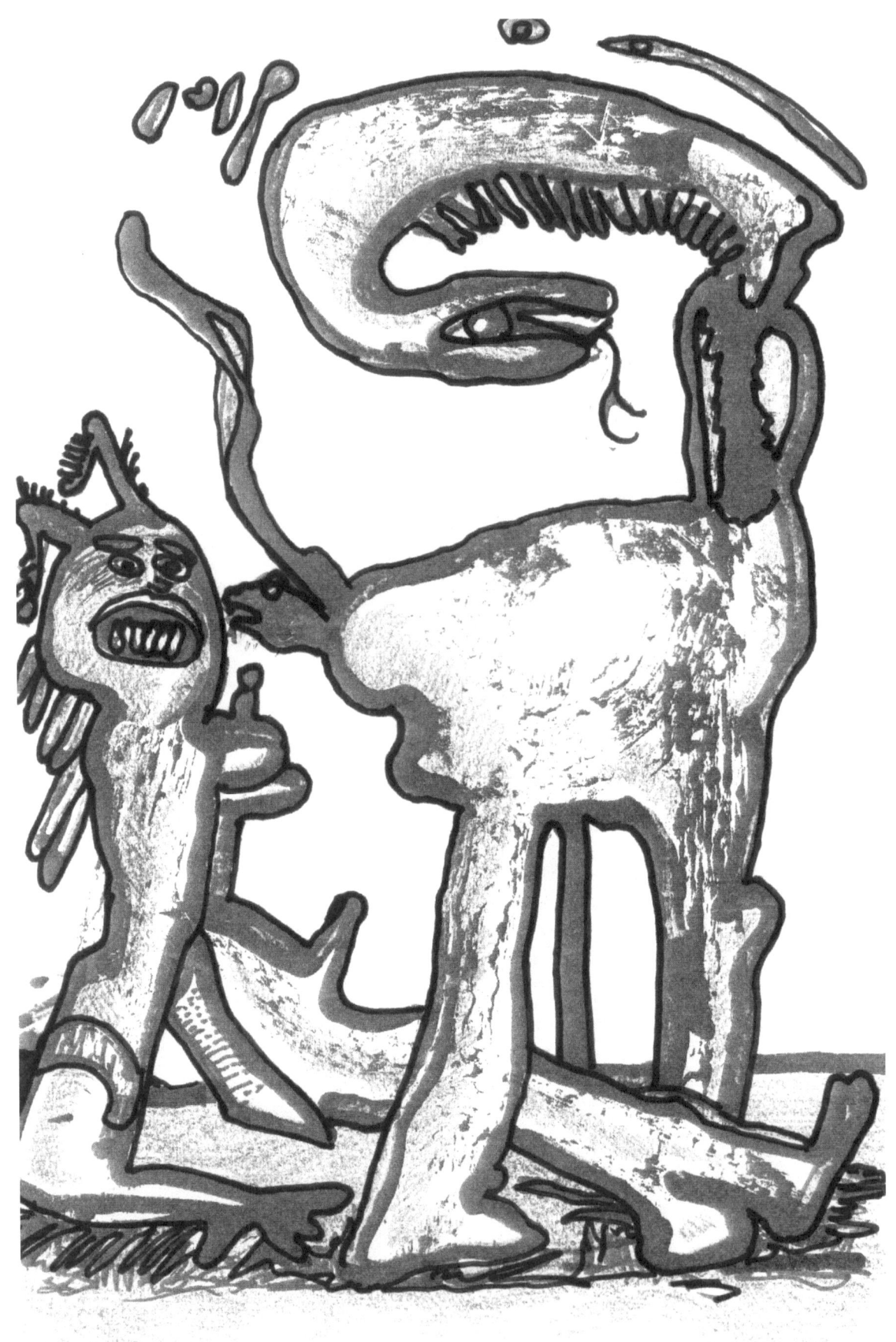

Plate 7: Up'ing the Ante

With Soul #2 "in the bag," Coyote is ready to nail the two Quasi boys Yow-Za and Yo-Ma-Ma, who have sadly ignored the plight of their sisters.

Coyote, offended by the perceived over-reaction of Sez Swan and her howling "you call that a Dick!" in front of everyone, was pissed. So pissed, in fact, that he chose a huge venomous snake shape for his next encounter. To enhance his terrorist posture, Coyote gives Yow-Za an actual face by which to see his tormentor!

Just to be cruel, Coyote also bestows arms that are used to prop up Yow-Za up to his ass level. With a huge whiff of coyote's "Soul," another snake comes out of what's left of Coyote's ass, and, before he can protest, sucks Yow-Za's soul deep within the gullet of his final form! Deep from within, a muffled "Holy Shit!" could be ascertained.

"Not really," chuckles Coyote, "Thanks just the same!"

Father Bendover, realizing the depth of Coyote's depravity, departs in a flurry of cactus and rocks, deciding to pass on the evening's planned "Busy butts" revival for his sex starved parish.

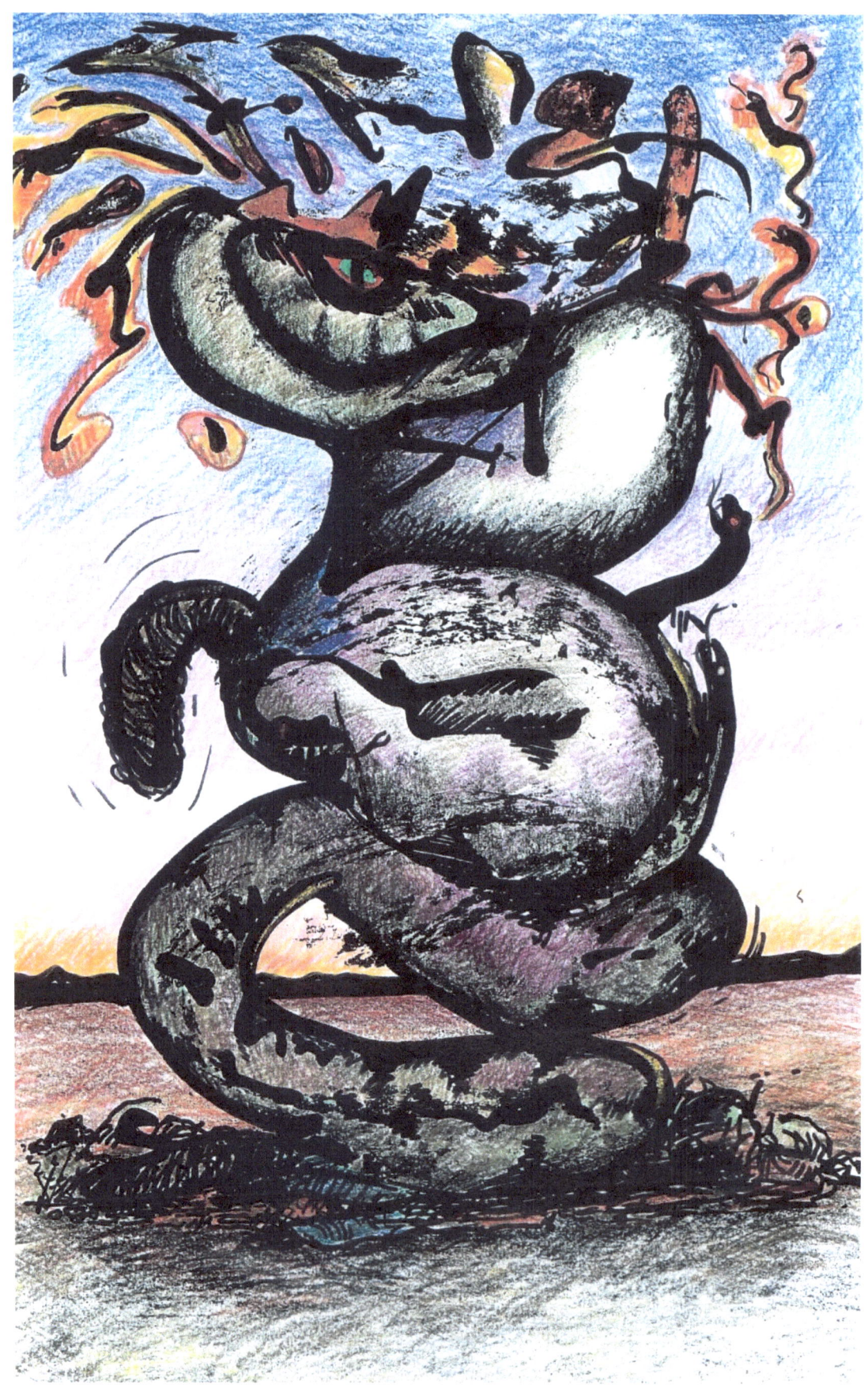

Plate 8: Long Lunch

Coyote is fully engulfed in his serpentine rendition chewing on the Soul of Yow-Za. In general, Coup De Vil and Father get the highest return when they cash out with the Big Guy.

Unfortunately, the snake routine has the drawback of highly toxic intestinal interference usually reserved for a cadaver.

For the last soul pluck, coyote will have to come up with a cleaner snatch if he doesn't want that seven pounds of Saca-Jah-Wee-Ah to get lost in the shuffle. Coup De Vil will be ecstatic with the girl scout Souls, but that picky-ass priest Father Bendover could be a problem.

Calling into play the Digestive Fast track (DFT) and Enzyme Suppression Protocol (ESP), coyote is able to spit out the lost mortal (Yow-Za) just in time to get the bounty and suit up for the final trawl, as seamen say.

Yo-Ma-Ma was sleeping by the fire unaware of the prowling shape-shifter's presence as he began the Mantra of Mayhem. The Final Trawl makes the desert seem almost real in its waterless oasis.

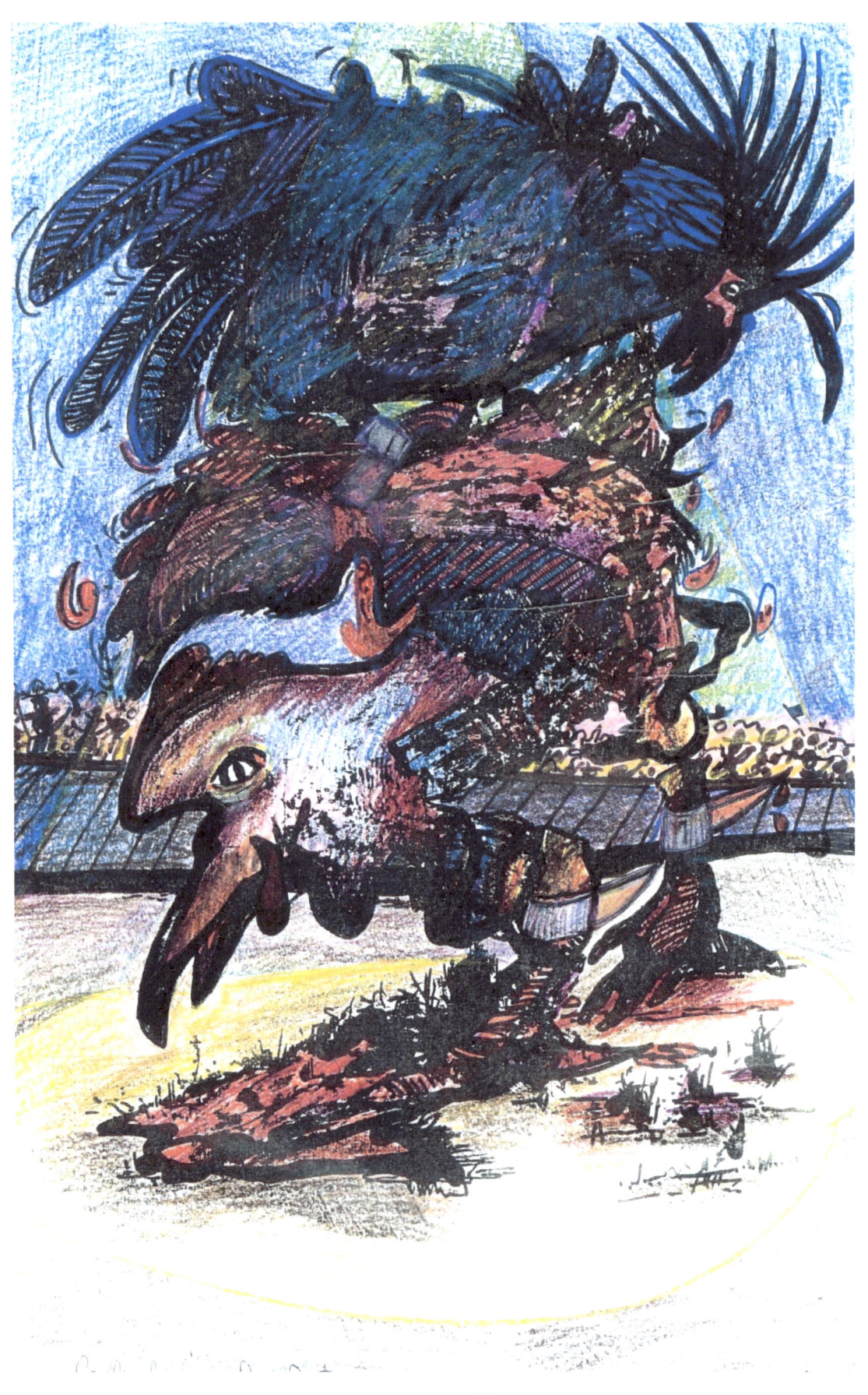

Plate 9: Fighting Back

Yo-Ma-Ma, the last celestial conscript of the Hadji-Badji road trip is not going to get Soul Plucked without (as feeble as it may seem) a fight. For this altercation, Coyote pulls up a shift to one of his favorite characters: Gall del Cielo, a valiant fighting cock from Casas Grande, Mexico, and for him: Zorro, a black monster bird from the San Diego onion fields. He is an ass-kicking feather-fowled gladiator ready for the Games to begin!!

Gallo del Cielo was stolen in Casas Grande and smuggled across the Rio Grande underneath the arm of Carlos Zaragoza. He had a cracked beak with one eye rolling crazy in his head. He looked like a derelict and everyone with their cherried-out fighting birds laughed when he pulled Gallo del Cielo out from underneath his coat. They all cried, later on, when Carlos walked away with a thousand dollar bill, and their birds were tossed out back of the ring with their throats slit by Gallo del Cielo's master gaffe.

Everything would have gone great except for the fact that the shape shift introduced a wuss into the great heart of the original Gall del Cielo. One who knew nothing of a life of fighting for one's life every other night until the inevitable bloody end.

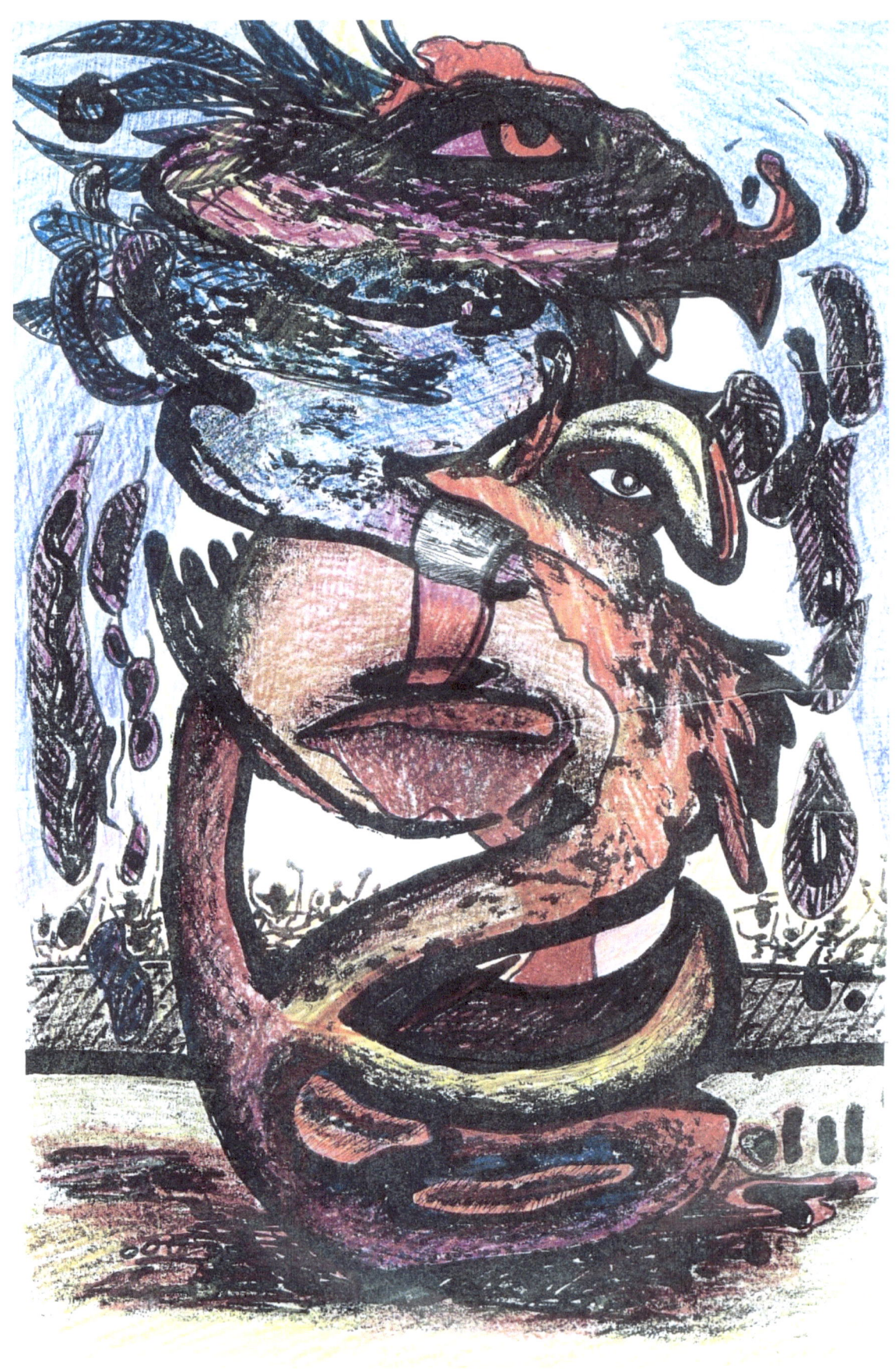

Plate 10: Bitter End

Zorro and Gallo del (now Yo-Ma-Ma), high above the fighting sands, flew at each other time and time again. And then, finally with one fierce slashing gasp, Zorro drove his gaffe deep into Gallo del Yo-Ma-Ma's heaving breast. Coyote stepped into snatch the fleeting soul of his dying bird shape before anyone figured out what had happened.

He flees like a ghost with his gunny sack full of Souls, heading back to the Valley of No with his loot. "Time to get High!" he hoots as he stops at a roadside hooch for a "cold one." That's right, coyotes love beer! Unfortunately, this was on a Reservation and he didn't have his spirit I.D. Pissed, he stomped out, unaware of the threat closing in behind him.

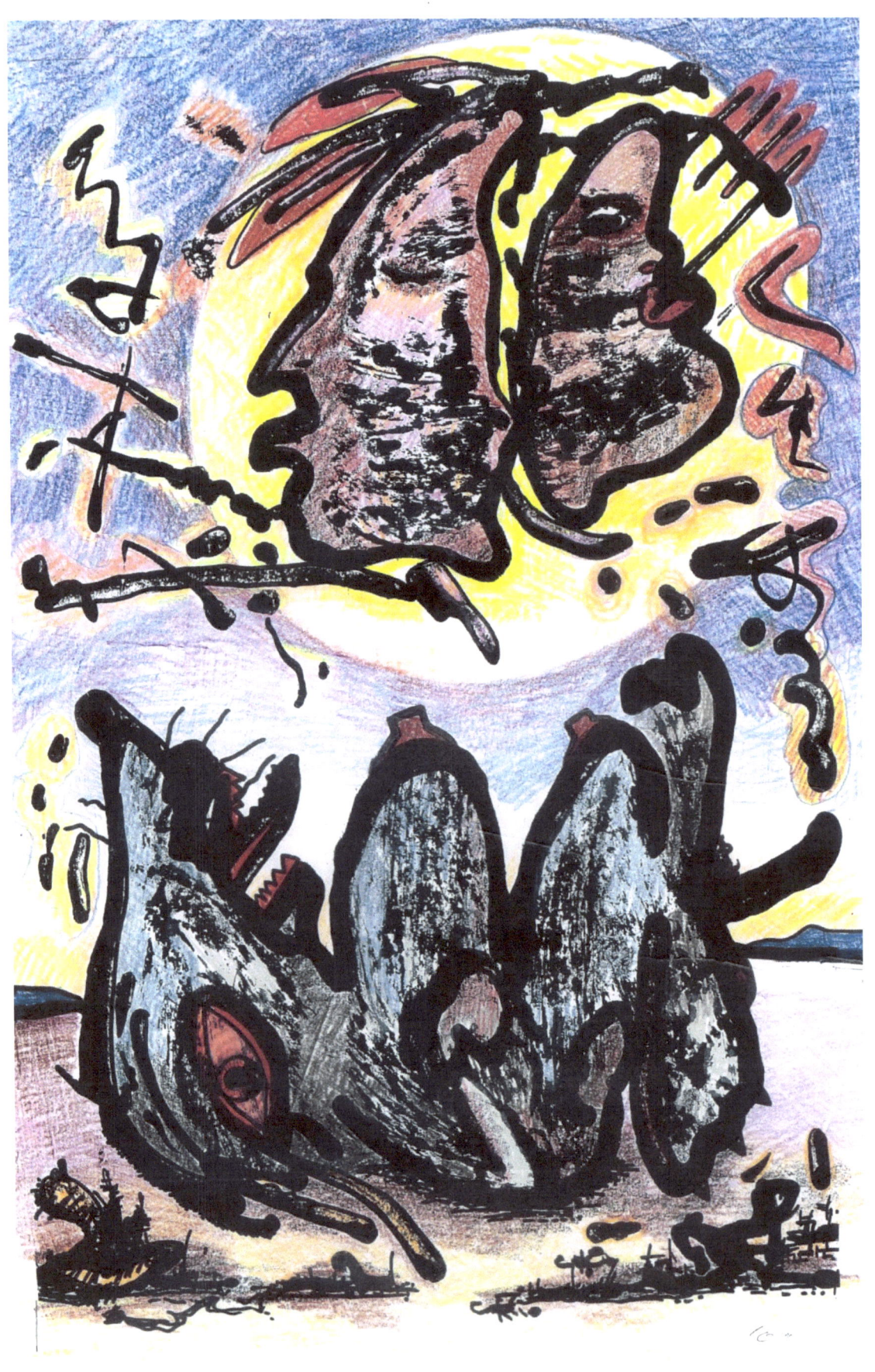

Plate 11: Justice

Dragging his bag of Souls behind him (you'd think they'd be lighter), Coyote is set upon by Spirit Forces of none other than Hermorpho and Dytee, guardians of the Hadji-Badjis on the road to the High Mesa.

Coyote squealing like a stuck pig, droops his loot, allowing his sack of Souls to escape to rejoin the physical world of Goh-Di-Gah, Sez Schwan, Yow-Za, and Yo-Ma-Ma with their new Spirit Guide Hoo-Dat-Se-Hoo-Dat to lead them onward to the High Mesa and the waiting Hogan of No-Na-Me.

Coyote, powerless and weak, receives his "Reward" for a life of malice, cruelty, perversion. None of that Baptist bullshit about "Hate the sin, Love the Sinner."

His big hairy barrel chest grows two huge double "D"s that drag the ground in constant pain as he runs crazy through the bush. His cantankerous old cock was turned into a cactus pole and right next to his ass grew a huge vagina. Now and for eternity Hermorpho-Coyote will roam the Wasteland fighting off the copulating efforts of all that lives there (especially those horny Nightwalkers) who have the right "equipment," or any "equipment" at all, for that matter.

So, the next time you're in the desert at night and Diableros begin their sacred dance, that howling noise you think is a coyote is none other than Coyote getting his cherry popped or an ass-breaking "Hello, ma cheri" from a fudgey-nudgey Nightwalker.

Raison d'Etre

by R.C. Webb

I began my study of painting and printmaking at East Carolina College in Greeneville, North Carolina, in the summer of '62. I had no interest in drawing or painting tobacco barns or other local color. Instead, I was drawn into the metaphysical paintings of deChirico, the critical paranoia of Dali, the visions of Tangy, and the automatisms of Miro, Klee, and Masson.

Intellectually, I was not involved with theory and made little sense of what Breton was telling the world about Surrealism. Being visually oriented, absorbing the power, form, and content of the painters--the Veristic wing of the Surrealist movement--came easily to me. I was seduced by those early mentors in the process of Surrealism, which became my life-long Raison d'Etre. My first Cause.

In 1970, I entered the so-called visionary cloisters of the San Francisco Art Institute. California in the early seventies was a hotbed of political and artistic upheaval against the Vietnam War. With activist roots in the Civil Rights Movement and the Anti-War Movement, I was no stranger to these radical manifestations. The Visionary School, besides being archaic, boring, and irrelevant to current events soon collapsed in the exciting drama of street riots, inflammatory speeches, and guerilla art actions.

The School of Ultra-Realism emerged, and though not yet politicized, it drove the final stake into the heart of the tenured super heroes of Modernism. The New Radicalism in Art was on the march!

A new critical criteria for the advancement of Revolutionary Art theory was put forth, which, in essence stated that revolutionary art must have content which accurately represents the relationship between Victim, Enemy, and Solution, or V.E.S., in any given situation. It was discovered, in the course of training the propaganda wings of certain organizations, that lessons had to be created that did not require any artistic talent, per se, on the part of the group members. It was then discovered that, by cutting images out of Class-oriented magazines, such as *Better Homes and Gardens, Harper's Bazaar, Vogue,* etc. and putting them in a layout with images from the Black Book of

Hunger, NACLA publications, and other radical sources, elements of syntax, such as tension, context, and proximity created intense psychological agitation. The addition of the Solution principal, depending on how violent or finite it was, was left to the particular group's philosophy and added the final touches to the work.

The V.E.S. principal soon had a following and evolved through dialogue, experimentation, and criticism into the School of Attack Surrealism. Although not a formal movement, more underground than not, kindred spirits were known, and not always to each other (for safety's sake), to be proliferating around the urban landscape from Los Angeles to Seattle, infiltrating and upstaging unworthy events, publishing violent manifestos, and most importantly, creating art in the V.E.S. genre.

The traditionally Surrealist technique of randomly combining seemingly obtuse visual elements to create a syntactical collapse to be replaced by a more powerful artistic idea served the propagandists well. By not signing up for any particular "Solution," it was possible to avoid being sucked into ill-fated plots, all night arguments about content, and political correctness. The resulting works, built around Cezanne's Composition, were concise, forceful testimony both to our Movement and ourselves, and to the unhappy recipients of our ideas.

All through the remaining war years, and even into the 80s and 90s, I continued, almost in a vacuum to create hard-hitting, issue-oriented imagery (Anti-Nuke, AIDS, Religious Right, etc.) to continue illuminating the processes of my Surrealism.

My belief in the philosophical core of a socially virulent Surrealism has never waned. The politically caustic image in its Surrealist trappings or "The Surrealism in service to the Revolution" (a cult classic) had, for the most part, run its course.

The "Attack" principle, like the Phoenix, has risen from the ashes of the Left in a more psychological form, and the "Victim," as well as the "Enemy" are also back on line. The only difference between the old and the new is the context. For example, the original "Victim" was a socially recognized entity. Now, the "Victim" is the viewer, with all their hysterical dysfunction and sexual hang-ups. The "Enemy" is nothing less than the sum total of the Artist's own megalomaniacal need to divide and conquer the rational intrusions of the viewer into the destructive/creative cycle.

The "Solution" is entirely plausible as the view is confronted with the sardonic, sarcastic, and satirical non-factual truth of Veristicism; a politically challenged set of sexual assumptions; and a virtual, user-friendly alphabet of psych-iconography stewing in a post-psychotropic universe easily pilfered by the confused and vulnerable observer for their own perverse titillation or for self-indulgent pathos in a bloodless, non-violent context.

Attack Surrealism has put teeth back in the words of Breton and who-knows-what in the pantaloons of Dali. The important thing is that, as members in good standing or not, they have reached immortality together, sniggering like whores in a butt-rash clinic who, in spite of their incredible discomfort, know things could be a hell of a lot worse!

As for me, I will always push the Visionary envelope, as part of the New Surrealism or not, to bring the contradictions between our radical history and the egocentric reality of our artistic lives into some type of historical focus, both as artists/humans and citizens of the World.

You can follow me @burnt_lunch or visit my literary-artistic websites at www.blackcatpublishing.blogspot.com and www.burntlunch.blogspot.com.

See my artwork at www.imagekind.com; just search for "webbsurrealism" to see my galleries.

www.ingramcontent.com/pod-product-compliance
Lightning Source LLC
Chambersburg PA
CBHW050414180526
45159CB00005B/2266